AT

NO ONE

1982 Agnes Lynch Starrett Poetry Prize

SHOUTING AT NO ONE

Lawrence Joseph

University of Pittsburgh Press

Published by the University of Pittsburgh Press, Pittsburgh, Pa. 15260
Copyright © 1983, Lawrence Joseph
All rights reserved
Feffer and Simons, Inc., London
Manufactured in the United States of America

Library of Congress Cataloging in Publication Data

Joseph, Lawrence.
  Shouting at no one.

  (Pitt poetry series)
  I. Title. II. Series.
PS3560.O775S5 1983   811'.54   82-20052
ISBN 0-8229-3478-7
ISBN 0-8229-5350-1 (pbk.)

The author would like to thank the editors of the publications in which the following poems, often in earlier versions, have appeared: "Is It You?" first appeared in *Commonweal.* "Fog," "In Each Cell of My Body," and "Louie, Son of Hanna Francis" originally appeared in the *Detroit Free Press.* "Encounter" was first published in *New York Quarterly.* "It Will Rain All Day" is reprinted courtesy of the *Michigan Quarterly Review.* "Even the Idiot Makes Deals" is reprinted from *New Letters.* "Do What You Can" and "Driving Again" are reprinted with permission from *The Ontario Review.* "I Think About Thigpen Again," "In the Tenth Year of War," and "It's Not Me Shouting at No One" are reprinted from *The Paris Review.* "The Phoenix Has Come to a Mountain in Lebanon" first appeared in *Poetry East.* "Before Going Back," "Then," and "When You've Been Here Long Enough" are reprinted with permission from *Stand* (Newcastle upon Tyne, England).

"I was appointed the poet of heaven" was included in a manuscript that received First Prize in the Major Poetry Division of the Avery and Jule Hopwood Award, 1970, and later appeared in *Broadsheet* (Cambridge, England). "When You've Been Here Long Enough" also appeared in *The Hopwood Anthology: Five Decades of American Poetry* (1981).

*The publication of this book is supported by grants
from the National Endowment for the Arts
in Washington, D.C., a Federal agency,
and the Pennsylvania Council on the Arts.*

For my father and mother

CONTENTS

I was appointed the poet of heaven.

It was my duty to describe
Theresa's small roses
as they bent in the wind.

I tired of this
and asked you to let me
write about something else.
You ordered, "Sit
in the trees where the angels sleep
and copy their breaths
in verse."

So I did,
and soon I had a public following:

Saint Agnes with red cheeks,
Saint Dorothy with a moon between her fingers
and the Hosts of Heaven.

You said, "You've failed me."
I told you, "I'll write lovelier poems,"
but, you answered,
"You've already had your chance:

you will be pulled from a womb
into a city."

I

THEN

Joseph Joseph breathed slower
as if that would stop
the pain splitting his heart.
He turned the ignition key
to start the motor and leave
Joseph's Food Market to those
who wanted what was left.
Take the canned peaches,
take the greens, the turnips,
drink the damn whiskey
spilled on the floor,
he might have said.
Though fire was eating half
Detroit, Joseph could only think
of how his father,
with his bad legs, used to hunch
over the cutting board
alone in light particled
with sawdust behind
the meat counter, and he began
to cry. Had you been there
you would have been thinking
of the old Market's wooden walls
turned to ash or how Joseph's whole arm
had been shaking as he stooped
to pick up an onion,
and you would have been afraid.
You wouldn't have known
that soon Joseph Joseph would stumble,
his body paralyzed an instant
from neck to groin.

You would simply have shaken your head
at the tenement named "Barbara" in flames
or the Guardsman with an M-16
looking in the window of Dave's Playboy Barbershop,
then closed your eyes
and murmured, This can't be.

You wouldn't have known
it would take nine years
before you'd realize the voice howling in you
was born then.

4

DRIVING AGAIN

Driving again,
this time Van Dyke Avenue.
Just beyond my window
October wind raises
a leaf from a sewer,
a gray-haired man standing in a crowd
before the Mount Zion Temple
tips his hat, "not bad, and you?"
When I was a child
I saw this church through the window
of a '51 Chevrolet
huddled beside my grandmother
in the backseat, her small
soft hands holding mine,
her perfume and the smell from squirrel
fur around her neck
spinning me to sleep.
Now I pass a woman,
her brown-blond face spotted purple,
who lowers her head
to spit, I see
a boy's words, "Dirty Killer Hood,"
in spray paint
on the wall of U.A.W. Local 89.
Where was it? I stumbled
through the darkness to the door
before I realized
I was waking from a dream
of this street, this smoke
from Eldon Axle foundry, these
motor blocks stacked against
this dull sky. Too many times

I stood on a loading dock
and watched morning air change
from red to iron.
"Gimme coffee, gimme a cigarette,"
a face asked me, "ain't no life,"
another warned.
Here is the cemetery.
Beneath stones engraved in Arabic
my grandfather, my grandmother.
Beneath this earth
grandpa whose sad eyes
could not endure
the pain of legs numbed
forever, grandma
who smiled although cells
crushed her brain.
Years ago, on a day like this,
I fell to my knees
with my father to pull grass
from their stones.
I did not cry.
When I closed my eyes I did not pray.
Now, in a car, on Van Dyke,
I cry for them and for me.

I HAD NO MORE TO SAY

The last time I saw her
this flat
above the 7-Up Cadillac Bar—
empty now, windows closed
and covered with dust—
was a coffee house
to which I came
because I knew she'd
be there.
At the window, away
from the others,
she told me about
her mother, always
alone, her father
somewhere else,
in a hotel, in a bar,
her sister who hated
everything.
I told her about
Dodge Truck.
How I swung differentials,
greased bearings,
lifted hubs to axle casings
in 110° heat.
How the repairman said nothing
as he watched me
almost lose two fingers.
Although she did
not answer, her face
tensed and her eyes
told me, Don't
be afraid, it
won't last forever.

I had no more to say.
I took her hand,
walked to the center
of the room. As voices
on the phonograph sang
we turned, descended
in one beat, rose,
shifted and shifted again.
I sang to her
like the song.
I forgot
what the morning
would bring: the early
bus ride, nervousness,
the factory.

HERE

Pockets puffed with bottles,
hair stiff, rising
in gray wind.
He comes to a dog without hair
sleeping in the weeds
near the old Packard plant,
reads "can't see"
in the dust of a window.
One April morning as
spiders walk on soft, black stones
and the colors of motor oil
spread in rainwater pools
I am where he is,
but I don't look him in the eyes,
I don't want to hold him and tell him Yes
if he asks something.
Above us white smoke
drifts with large dark clouds
toward old Poletown,
where the houses are gone.
Now it is September
and I am there, between
the silhouette of broken fences
and weeds with yellow hair
seizing their own piece of buried sun.
Rain streams down my face,
a poplar breathes
over the only house I can see,
burned and gutted.
The only sign of human life
is the crashing sound
of a bottle thrown hard on cement,
east of this wasteland,
where the towers smoke.

BETWEEN US

What was his name?
Drank gin from
a used paper cup, wasn't
even break time yet.
Sitting on a Hi-Lo, his
muscled arms hung
over the wheel.

Between us
white dust covered
with sulphur, the dream
of a farm.
"In a few years ought to have
five head of cattle
and a tractor."

9 years and 283 miles
to the south side, the voices
in the Whole Truth Mission
singing gospel. "But I
came right here to
Mt. Elliott Street.
Wasn't no future
praisin' Jesus."

I THINK ABOUT THIGPEN AGAIN

I think about Thigpen again.
On the floor in an apartment
on Boston Boulevard, he knows
he's going to die.
I see the record of the criminal court.
Thigpen opens the door,
sees a gun in his face,
pleads, "I don't have
nothing to do with this!"
According to the pathologist
death was caused
by massive tissue destruction,
contusion and swelling of the brain.
In the county morgue
Thigpen's father whispered,
"That's my baby son."
And what must have been said after was,
"You the wrongest person
in the wrongest place,
the wrongest time, Thig."
That was eleven years ago.
Sixteen years ago he stuffed
a basketball into the face
of the Brother Rice forward
who called him a name, and we
went wild. I saw him
in Louis the Hatter's, downtown.
He pointed at my Stetson,
laughed, "You ain't ever
gonna look like a nigger."
Later, he wrote poems of babies
in frozen tenements,

garbage alive with maggots,
the love a woman makes,
the greasy riders with Detroit skin,
the toughest in the world.

He would be the poet of this hell.

That bullet slicing your brain
isn't poetry, Thigpen.

IT WILL RAIN ALL DAY

Breakfast at Buck's Eat Place;
a portrait of Henry Ford,
two eggs, hash browns,
sour coffee. Afterwards
I walk out on Vernor Avenue,
"looks like a river in the rain,"
the signs from small stores hanging
over the wet sidewalks like trees.
But rivers are not passed over
by a woman wearing a windbreaker
with flags sewn on both shoulders,
muttering to herself, head down,
or an unshaven man older
than he is, his body slanting
as if he's about to fall
headlong into a dream.
Neither looks at me waiting
at the light, in my car,
as windshield wipers eliminate
the stars of water.
Along the cemetery, poplars
look upward with thousands
of eyes into the rain
that comes down on hills of lime
and coal, reminding me of Metz,
but the wind
that lifted rhododendrons that April
isn't here with me. What
do I want, driving through streets
past bars where fifty-year-old
truck drivers sip whiskey
and don't feel like talking,

13

past houses where chimney smoke
reveals fires and rooms I will
never know? On Fort Street
I pass the bar with "Fight Poverty—
Drink & Dance" scrawled in white paint
across its windowless front,
and then a block-long building,
windows knocked in, wires ripped
from the walls, toilet bowls
covered with dirt and spiderwebs.
It will rain all day.
I see a large crane lifting
a railroad car, piles of bald tires,
the two towers of Saint Anne's
where, in a corner, there are crutches,
body braces and letters written
to acknowledge miracles. I want
all this to come to an end
or a beginning, I want to look
into the black eyes of the lone woman
waiting for a bus and say
something, I want my memory
to hold this air, so I can make
the hills with white hair
and the clouds breaking into blackness
my own, carry them with me
like the letters and icons
immigrants take in suitcases
to strange countries.

BEFORE GOING BACK

Shot five times in the chest
with a .38, only a boy,
member, the Black Killers gang,
on the table in the Emergency Room,
drugged, gasping, tube rammed
through his windpipe for ventilation.
Tube through which you breathed
for him after you cracked
and spread his chest with a knife
and bone cutters, cross-clamped
the descending aorta, held
and massaged his heart,
oversewed holes in the right ventricle
and holes at the hilum
of the lung and tied his chest
with yards of silk, blood
on your face and hands
and hair, blood soaked
through socks and shoes before
it rushed down the drain.
Now you pace the Receiving Dock,
breathe the hot July air,
its trace of sulphur, hear its sirens
coming toward you.
You shake your head to shake
away your headache. You don't
ask why you remember the man
your father said was "down
on his luck," his face fallen,
two overcoats opened
to frozen wind, his arm lifted
to announce words only he hears,

or why you remember the night
you got out of your car,
walked through the small crowd
outside the liquor store
just because, you thought later,
you needed to walk by them all
without looking any of them
in the eye or speaking,
you don't think "must
be past midnight," because
it doesn't matter what
is remembered, it doesn't matter
what time it is. What matters
is the boy will live.
He'll waken, his voice
hushed. You'll be the first one
to tell him he'll never talk again,
that he'll have to walk
with a cane. He'll cry. He'll
never know how you paced
this Dock before going back
to wipe sweat from his forehead
and whisper words he didn't hear.

NOT YET

When my father breathed
unevenly I breathed
unevenly, I prayed
in St. Maron's Cathedral
for the strength
of a cedar tree
and for the world to change.
When I saw my father's tears
I did not pray;
I hated our grocery store
where the bullet
barely missed his heart,
I hoped the mists exhaled
by the Vale of Esk
in a country of lakes
4,000 miles away
would be mine.
That was before
Lopez whispered through his rotten teeth
behind a maze of welding guns,
"You're colored, like me,"
before I knew
there is so much
anger in my heart,
so much need
to avenge the holy cross
and the holy card
with its prayers for the dead,
so many words
I have no choice to say.

Years without enough to make me
stop talking!
I want it all.
I don't want
the angel inside me, sword in hand,
to be silent.
Not yet.

II

THE PHOENIX HAS COME
TO A MOUNTAIN IN LEBANON

1

I was a child when the wolves came
from the north and ate our donkey.
My father shouted so much
I was afraid. I hid
in the heavy mountain grass
where he could not see me.
When it was dark I went back to the house.
He was not there.
My mother was on her knees
praying before the bag of silkworm eggs
that hung from the ceiling.

2

I was the kind of boy who prayed
before a statue's face,
sorry for all the tears
that were for me
because I was "always
inside out."

Again and again
I climbed above the village
to think about
what obsessed me:
the tax collectors who melted
the iron points of our plows
into guns, the shrapnel
I saw in my cousin's stomach;
to repeat to myself
what my brother's letter said:
"it is better here,
there is work, there is money
in these factories."

3

I stand over a dead body
and feel nothing
for the bones I've crushed:
my bones have been
crushed for centuries.
I fire my rifle into the sun,
shout God's name,
return to ruins to roast a lamb.
I will eat the head
first and then the bowels.
I will drink wine
until I cannot
see the dream of my own land.

4

The Phoenix has come
to a mountain
in Lebanon, its red flesh
breathing the sun,
breathing myrtle and poppies,
the prayers and wailing,
breathing the singing
Dog River and the Bridge
of Stone.
The Phoenix
is dying
and has come to be
what the land is,
wanting the eyes that no longer
listen, the widow's hair
on fire, wanting the stars
that do not touch
the stones.
The winds are dry
and do not
cool its burning;
the rains will not be
its new blood now.
Filled with the final words
of those left in a ditch
to die, with the black skin
of the bald woman
who's cried almost every day
for eighty years,
filled with the river at whose mouth
a thousand wars began,

river gone now into rock
and crystal after giving
the world its wheat,
the Phoenix
breathes,
goes down the mountain
to the burning cities,
to the sea
where a long boat waits to sail
to another world.

YOU ONLY EXIST INSIDE ME

Where Dix Highway ends
long boats tug ore
across a green canal.
In a cafe, Yemenites
cheat at dice
and talk about whores.
You drink coffee,
smoke, remember
a room, a table
that held the weight
of your elbows,
the small notebook
in which you wrote
"our labor put the world on wheels";
one day someone
will find it and think
of thick-lipped buckets,
iron pigs growing
into billets.
Alone, I walk this street
of ice, making this up:
you only exist inside me.
A siren blows.
It is 3:30.
I remember how
I punched the clock.
My legs jerked into full stride
toward a room.
I sat at a table
rubbing my eyes.

I did not feel.
I did not think.

LOUIE, SON OF HANNA FRANCIS

Catches the bus
at the corner
of Seminole and Charlevoix,
takes it past
the smell of bread, grinding
dynamos, yellow
streetlight,
Our Lady of Redemption
Melchite Catholic Church,
transfer
north at McDougall,
transfer downtown at
Gratiot, get off
at Russell, not yet
6 o'clock,

Louie,
son of Hanna Francis,
descendant of Sem,
of the land Aram Naharaim
where, between two rivers,
soil is soft and black, good
for tomatoes, eggplant, corn,

says to himself, Buy
sausage from Hammond-Standish,
buy produce, but
no cauliflower, from
Caramagno, as he
walks in dark
drops of water dissolving
on his sun-colored face.

ENCOUNTER

Face lowered in his collar,
he leans back
against the darkness
of a boarded doorway.
A flame larger
than the sun
pours from a thin pipe.
Miles of factory
heaped to the half red
and half black sky
glow in his thin eyes.

    He steps out
into the frozen wind,
the only strip of light
breaks, scatters
behind him down the alley.
Says he knows
everything: the mysteries
of motors, how to get
easy jobs in the shop,
numbers, the streets,
where you can go
under a bridge at night
in a small boat, unnoticed.

FOG

All day the air was fog;
couldn't see
the barbed wire, rusting
scraps, stacks
and stacks of pallets,
the tarpaper roof
of Dreamer's shack,
the underground
caverns of salt hardening
around bones.

     The fog says,
Who will save
Detroit now?
A toothless face
in a window shakes No,
sore fingers
that want to be still
say, Not me.
Not far away from where
Youmna lies
freezing in bed,
rolling her eyes, declaring,
This is a place!
the remains of mountains
wait to be moved
through smokestacks
into air.

ALL DAY

At four in the morning
already walking
up Orleans
to Eastern Market, two,
three miles away,
a burlap bag
over his shoulder,
the rows of wooden houses
asleep. Behind
him, low horns
on the river, a full moon
casting moist
blue light; ahead, the sounds
of cars and trucks
on Vernor Highway;
above, oak branches
turning in the high winds.

All day he drops the silver
into a cigar box;
the pennies he puts
in a jar. He gives
too much credit
and the markings on
small, torn pieces
of paper bag will be
forgotten. At dusk
he fills the bag again—
with eggplant, squash,
the last pieces of shank—
and goes
to the houses he knows
don't have enough,

saying nothing
as he gives, shaking his head
if someone starts to speak.

When the bag is empty
he walks
through the black streets
past faces rocking
on the porches. The shouts
of the children in the alley
and he's home, to Mary,
Katherine, Anne, Matry,
Isabelle, Sabe, Josephine,
Helen, Genevieve, Basily,
and Barbara. The screen door
slams behind him.
Unnoticed, he sits down
to unlace his shoes,
to rub his sore feet.
He leans back, his eyes
close, his head
begins to nod at the voices
in the kitchen; he sees,
a world away,
the salamander sliding
down a rock, stars
dropping behind mountains
into the sea.

HE IS KHATCHIG GABOUDABIAN

1

He hears screams in the alley:
a cousin cuts a cousin's throat.
"We are all cousins," they say,
but they are not his cousins,
these black men from Yemen,
curved daggers cinched to their waists,
who kill for women.
He coughs, wakens suddenly.
Is this a dream? What time is it?
Noon? He lifts the shade:
it is past noon; the smoke
from the plant is heavy, red,
the day is gray again.
He walks across his room,
lights a cigarette, sits down on the bed,
gets up, walks, sits down again.
His legs hurt; doctor says
his blood is bad. What time is it?
He's hungry. He scratches his ribs.
He must not forget to take his pills.

2

Before he is born
because there is no work in Sivis
his father crosses the border
into Bulgaria forever.
War brings soldiers with long rifles
who take his mother, brothers
and sister away forever.
In Arabkir he is an orphan among orphans,
in Detroit an uncle sends him money
to come tap the cupola, pour
liquid metal into the ladle.

When I heard about their bodies
floating in a river of blood
you might say my heart was broke.
I was lost, there was no one
to tell me I was lost.
I used to pray beneath the cross
before I thought of all this,
before I thought.

3

He doesn't know how old he is,
he doesn't know his real name.

He knows pain crosses his shoulders.
His lungs cough blood.
He is dying.

He can't eat because he doesn't have
teeth and his gums bleed.
His room in the Hotel Salina doesn't have
heat and the pipes freeze
like the water in the toilet down the hall.

He complains to whomever listens
or doesn't listen
or to himself
if there is no one to complain to.

He is a well-known
loser at *barbouda,* a socialist
who speaks with arms and elbows.
He's ashamed to say he's sacrificed
women and family
to serve two masters: Henry Ford and dice.

4

The warm white wind, the afternoon light
feel the face of the man who knows he is dying.

His legs don't hurt as much.
He inhales without coughing.

A newspaper, sunglasses, a pack of cigarettes,
a hat, the clothes on his back,
a chair by a table in a coffee house, a window,
are his.
He can drink eight cups of coffee,
he can figure the importance
of Albania to Afghanistan.

This is where the world is!
Those who don't understand this don't understand!

He used to walk beside tons of sand,
storage bins, along the boat slip.
He remembers the dusk sun
golden across the black Rouge River.
He promises himself he will go there
one more time, one more time
to feel the power of earth, water, and sun
together, holding him.

5

In Salina, South Dearborn,
the air is cold, damp, deep
black and red, filled
with sulphur and the earth
roaring inside machines.
Crowds of young men on the street
shake and nod their heads,
waiting for the midnight shift.
If they do not acknowledge him
he does not care:
he is Khatchig Gaboudabian.
If he must shut himself in his room alone
he will.

I have the mind.
That will save me.

NOTHING AND NO ONE
AND NOWHERE TO GO

I've laughed before no one,
cried before fire floating
in iron molds, felt
the crow and the peppergrass
against brown dawn.
I never pray "Father" or "Son,"
I scavenge if I have to.
At Hudson Motorcar
an Iraqi I worked with
never talked, except
after the shift began,
he'd kneel and sing
"Allah la ilah." He wanted
mercy, from somewhere
in Arabia, but I never
wanted anything
from the metal rushing
into sand troughs
or the grease
I smelled and breathed.
I've always waited:
for warm rain to wash the sky,
for the woman
beside the river of sludge
to disappear.
Now I wait for the hours left,
alone, shivering,
wait until I can't
hear myself talking to myself
or hear my heart beat
for nothing and no one
and nowhere to go.

STOP TALKING TO YOURSELF!

There is always steam pouring from manholes,
there are always smokestacks heaving poison.

There is a dog behind the "Chez Paree Hotel"
kicking its hind legs, foaming at the mouth.

On a porch with Doric columns, a boy spits
into the wind. He wears a Borsalino hat.

Hands in his coat pockets, he wants you to know
he carries a gun. Old man on Bellevue Street

who came here believing the Five Dollar Day,
no teeth, cigarette hanging from his lower lip,

opens a barbed wire gate before a stone mansion.
You hear your voice. You don't remember speaking.

Stop talking to yourself! Be disciplined!
Look away from Our Lady of Lourdes

appearing to a statue of Bernadette beside
the brick warehouse with "Baby Pimp Dog" painted

across its wall. Forget the Albanian gypsy
whose hatred you feel as you stare into her eyes.

Do as you always do to convince yourself: recite
the "Our Father" and "Hail Mary" out loud, in Latin.

THERE IS A GOD
WHO HATES US SO MUCH

I

I was pulled from the womb
into this city.

I learned words when my grandfather
lost both legs.

Before the altar of God
I spent hours on my knees.
I felt God's anger
when my semen spilled into my hand.
I ate God's body.
I promised to never sin.

I learned sadness from my mother's eyes.
I learned silence in the dust
a woman hid behind
to cover her face of scars.
I learned blood from my father
fallen to a wooden floor,
a thief's bullet inside him.
He lived to warn me to forget.

After that I sucked darkness.

II

Years were a breath.

Alone, with whirring metal,
clattering and pounding
I could not abstract,
smells that tortured me,
I felt my words close inside me
like marrow.

I was a system of laws
I hated, a boy
afraid of burning
in a city that was burning
as my father cried
and my mother whispered in my hair.

III

I am the poet of my city.

I am the earth that burns the air,
those who talk to themselves,
blood and grease on hands.
I need to know
why I do not want to remember.

In dreams I run through streets
terrified, away
from mouths that hate me,
my face washed with fear.
In dreams I kill
so I will not be killed.

The city is the shadow
strapped to my back.

I am the poet of that shadow.

IV

Mother says, "Don't
think about it too much."

Father splashes cold water on his face,
vomits his nightmare:
he sweat before a man
who wanted to kill him.

I hold a holy candle and a palm branch,
kiss the feet of a statue,
drink holy water,
imagine my body without words,
pray to be able to sacrifice
like the saint
with arrows in his heart.

God gives the world
the brown and black frost
the city climbs through
to stars no one can see.

V

That is where I am now, in this city
where there are hours of sun
above the horizon and dirt in the air
that makes me want to holler.

There is a God who hates us so much:
we are given ears to hear ribs kicked in,
we are given eyes to see eyes close
before a city that burns itself to death.

Father shouts until his throat cracks,
the river stops in its sludge,
I pray to know what to pray for:
there is a God who hates us so much.

I was born in this city and live in this city
and know this city like no one else.
Who makes me eat my words and makes my eyes pain:
I measure you according to your creation.

IN THE TENTH YEAR OF WAR

I bend
over the machine. Heat
and oil
tune my inner ear. I'm
not ashamed, I
hang my head in
anticipation. Father,
steel smooth and silver,
make my brain new,
Jesus, the dirt on the walls
is coming from my body,
and love,
the spirit coming from your body—
everywhere you look now,
everything you touch,
it's good.
When,
in the tenth year of war
I prayed for help
and no one came,
I danced before the machine.

IS IT YOU?

Where the giant magnet lifts
pig iron and bales of steel
and a larva dangles
from a spider's thread
beside an old press machine,
where the '53 DeSoto is
among piles of chassis
and transmissions,
and air is wakened
by an ore boat's horn,

someone calls.
Is it you?, who numbers stars
the same as Job's
and hides words in my bones
demanding, Count them?
Is it you, calling me,
your blackest rib?

WHEN YOU'VE BEEN HERE
LONG ENOUGH

You breathe yellow smoke, you breathe lead
beside the river, talking out loud to no one.

A rat slips by you into the cold green water.
No longer, at 6 o'clock Mass, do you kneel,

body bent over and swaying, chanting,
"Mea culpa, mea culpa, mea maxima culpa,"

offering your sorrow to the Poor Souls in Purgatory,
no longer do you dream of your mother as a child

waiting for a streetcar in the snow, praying
to St. Jude to cure her sister's paralyzed hand.

When the waitress argues, "What you do is
hang them, downtown, in Grand Circus Park—

that would keep them off the streets," you don't answer.
You hear about the woman who 25 years ago touched

the back of your head and said, "It's shaped
just like your daddy's." She just sat there

and watched blood spray from her cut wrist all over
her room in the La Moon Manor Hotel. You just

shake your head. You're not surprised.
Because, when you've been here long enough

no one can make you believe the Black Cat
Dream Book provides your winning number.

Heaven answers your prayers with dust and you swallow it.
Alone, early morning, on the Wyoming Crosstown bus,

you feel the need to destroy, like everyone else,
as the doors open and no one comes on.

JUST LIKE YOU

Just like you
I hate
the boy with rotten teeth
who bites his lip, smiles,
"I didn't do it,"
just like you
I curse
my shit and want to dance
on the Board of Directors' oak table
in the Tower of Glass.
Bless me,
Father, for I have sinned:
I tell lies,
I don't pray.
I believe
the woman who shows me her artificial eye,
I prophesy
at noon gray sky will fall.
Just like you
burned earth burns my brain.
Not even a relic
touched to a relic
of the One True Cross
balances me.

IN EACH CELL OF MY BODY

When the world was born
I saw God
in the wind, with wings,
move into earth
and sleep.

In that life
I stared at mirages,
the roofs of shacks,
above them white water and sky,
Mama always saying, "That's
all he does."

In each cell of my body
is a morning: my sister
bleeds as she sleeps,
the old man comes home, arms
speckled with grease,
the scent of opening elm buds
hangs in the air,
and 27 silver stacks
push smoke
under a sky of rain clouds.

DO WHAT YOU CAN

In the Church of I AM she hears there is a time to heal,
but her son, Top Dog of the Errol Flynn gang,

doesn't lay down his sawed-off shotgun,
the corn she planted in the field where

the Marvel Motor Car factory once was
doesn't grow with pigweed and cockleburr.

When someone in the Resurrection Lounge laughs,
"Bohunk put the 2-foot dogfish in the whore's hand,"

someone's daughter whispers, "Fuck you,"
places a half-smoked cigarette in her coat pocket,

swings open the thick wooden door and walks
into air that freezes when it hears frost

coming from Sault Sainte Marie. Driving, I see
a shed of homing pigeons, get out of my car to look.

I answer, "What you care?" to a woman who shouts, "What you
    want?"
Beside the Church of St. John Nepomocene

an old man, hunched and cold, prays, "Mother of God"
to a statue of the Virgin Mary

surrounded by a heart-shaped rosary
of 53 black and 6 white bowling balls.

Where the Ford and Chrysler freeways cross
a sign snaps, 5,142,250,

the number of cars produced so far this year in America.
Not far away, on Beaufait Street,

a crowd gathers to look at the steam
from blood spread on the ice. The light red,

I press the accelerator to keep the motor warm.
I wonder if they know

that after the jury is instructed
on the Burden of Persuasion and the Burden of Truth,

that after the sentence of 20 to 30 years comes down,
when the accused begs, "Lord, I can't do that kind of time,"

the judge, looking down, will smile and say,
"Then do what you can."

EVEN THE IDIOT MAKES DEALS

On Mack Avenue the smell of hot iron closes your eyes:
you've chosen a city that moans in its dirt.

You memorize prayers in Arabic and forget them.
You memorize Statutes of Frauds and forget them.

You remember a boy with a knife who wanted money
from the Joseph Food Market safe. Sixteen years later

your uncle tells how he wakens, sweating, shaking,
"don't kill me," as the knife cuts his throat again.

He shows you the scar; it's healed.
"You learn how to forget," he reminds you.

You can't forget the boy who beats a woman to death
for money he could just have taken. His bones,

our bones, crumble in this damp, cold haze.
Even the idiot makes deals. She'll sell you her hair.

She wants you to look at her pocked face and her drool.
She knows you'll put a coin into her waiting hand.

IT'S NOT ME SHOUTING AT NO ONE

Before dawn, on the street again,
beneath sky that washes me
with ice, smoke, metal.
I don't want to think
the bullet pierced my shoulder,
the junkie's rotten teeth
laughed, his yellow hair froze.
I'm careful: I smoke
Turkish tobacco cigarette butts,
I drink a lot to piss a lot,
I fry the pig in its own fat,
eat the knuckles, brain, and stomach;
I don't eat the eyes!
Always four smokestacks
burning bones, somewhere
tears that won't stop,
everywhere blood becomes
flesh that wants to say something.
It's not me shouting at no one
in Cadillac Square: it's God
roaring inside me, afraid
to be alone.

PITT POETRY SERIES

Ed Ochester, General Editor